Gemini's
REFLECTION

Poetry By

Shiroma Perera-Nathan
& Sasheeka Costa

Thank you to all who have encouraged us to write and put this together, especially Peter for his advice and editing, Cindy for her encouragement, Luke for putting it together and Marie for the direction. Special thanks to those who believed in us and inspired these words.

To my first love, teacher
and loving grandmother, Leela Kumari.
—Shiroma Perera-Nathan

To each of you who has taught me about love, life,
heartbreak and disappointment — thank you.
You have been my muse and inspiration.
— Sasheeka Costa

A perfit description of the Cælestiall Orbes,

according to the moſt auncient doctrine of the
Pythagoreans, &c.

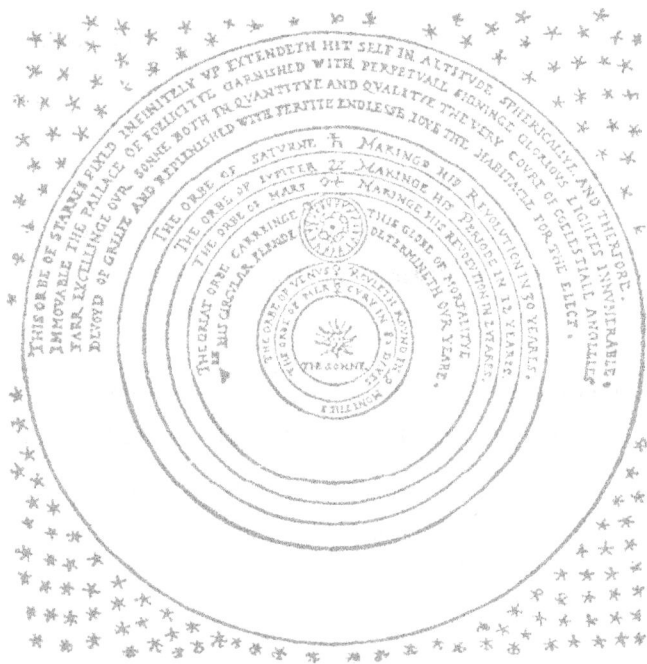

THIS ORBE OF STARRES FIXED INFINITELY VP EXTENDETH HIT SELF IN ALTITVDE SPHERICALLYE, AND THERFORE IMMOVABLE THE PALLACE OF FOELICITYE GARNISHED WITH PERPETVALL SHININGE GLORIOVS LIGHTES INNVMERABLE, FARR EXCELLINGE OVR SONNE BOTH IN QVANTITYE AND QVALITYE THE VERY COVRT OF CELESTIALL ANGELLES DEVOYD OF GRIEFE AND REPLENISHED WITH PERFITE ENDLESSE IOYE THE HABITACLE FOR THE ELECT.

THE ORBE OF SATVRNE ♄ MAKINGE HIS REVOLVTION IN 30 YEARES.

THE ORBE OF IVPITER ♃ MAKINGE HIS REVOLVTION IN 12 YEARES.

THE ORBE OF MARS ♂ MAKINGE HIS REVOLVTION IN 2 YEARE.

THE GREAT ORBE CARRYINGE THIS GLOBE OF MORTALITYE IN HIS CIRCVLAR PERIODE DETERMINETH OVR YEARE.

THE ORBE OF VENVS ♀ REVOLVTH IN 9 MONTHS.

THE ORBE OF ☿ CVRSVS IN 88 DAYES.

THE SONNE.

INTRODUCTION

The Gemini Woman

Though she managed to pick plenty of beautiful rushes as the boat glided by, there was always a more lovely one that she couldn't reach. "The prettiest ones are always further!" she said at last, with a sigh at the obstinacy of the rushes in growing so far off.
— Sun Signs, Linda Goodman

The authors were both born under the celestial sign of Gemini, represented by the twins Castor and Pollux, and ruled by Mercury, the planet of communication. Gemini's artistic preference is poetry and is represented by the household item — a mirror. Geminis are often thought to have a dual personality, the ability to see both sides of an issue and have many aspects to them.

Reflection has a double meaning — on one hand it is an image we see in the mirror and yet it's also an idea to which we give expression.

The authors found that they had written pieces of verse over the years which when they shared with each other felt connected. Certain pieces matched, others showed opposite meanings or common themes.

In Geminis' Reflection we hope to share with you, our dear reader, our collection of reflections on our existence; life, love, friendship, death, goals, despair, obsessions, and learning, via verse our preferred means of communicating. If you look more closely, you may have your own connection.

Shiroma Perera-Nathan   Sasheeka Costa

Ink bleeding truth
Mind's eye melting into words
Soul lays bare
To be worthy of only the other

To know is to understand the bleeding
The heart aches to be united with her partner

Celestial twins doomed never to find each other
So she bleeds alone
In the eternal hope
Surely they will one day meet

But to what end?

TWINS

Uninvited, you moved into my head
Now my every waking thought is of you
I go about my day and you are there
I try to sleep but even then you linger
I try to evict you but you will not leave

Unexpected, you settled into my heart
Making me want to give up everything for you
Making me yearn to give you things I do not even have
Making me love you without rhyme
Making me need you without reason

But you are not here where I need you to be
My arms long for you but they are destined to be empty
My soul craves my mate but in vain
And my lips, they are separated from their twin

She breathed when there was no air
To give to those she held dear
She could have been someone
She did not know how
In a suffocating antipodal world
She finds it hard to move
She is not visible
Will this pass too?

And so she slept even though the sun shone
As her children played
Hoping to awake to the answer
Her brown pools of desperation opened
To a wound deeper
And numbness took over

Feelings were of no use
Each attempt another failure
Who said there was a rainbow at the end?
She only found an ocean that drowned her
And the mermaid who took her there

DEPTH

We walked the road to heartbreak
Starting the day that we met
And soon we reached our destiny
A place named regret
It wasn't where we planned to go
Feeling alone and bereft
A matching pair of memories
Was all that we had left

Pieces of me he chiseled away
Take pride in his masterpiece of con artistry
When did the awareness come darling?
As Ella gave away her wisdom; that is when it dawned

Hope was a long gone illusion
Stolen by him with no regret
How long did you stare at the ticking clock darling?
Till he chipped the final piece with the knife of disillusionment:
that is when it stopped ticking

Fake facades take too much energy
When he pushed me to wear the mask of disheartenment
What made you discard the forced smile darling?
Until it was still believed, still believed echoed;
that is when I dropped it

Took as much as I could carry
Including heavy tears muffled by my salty pride
When did the floodgates open darling?
As I lay in agonizing solitude by the edge of world's end;
that is when it poured

And when the ebony night swallowed the blood moon
I packed the bags of yesterday with passion blooming
When did you decide to leave darling?
As the twilight door opened into an awakening;
That is when I rose

BROKEN

If you only knew
How every word I write
Contains a little piece of you

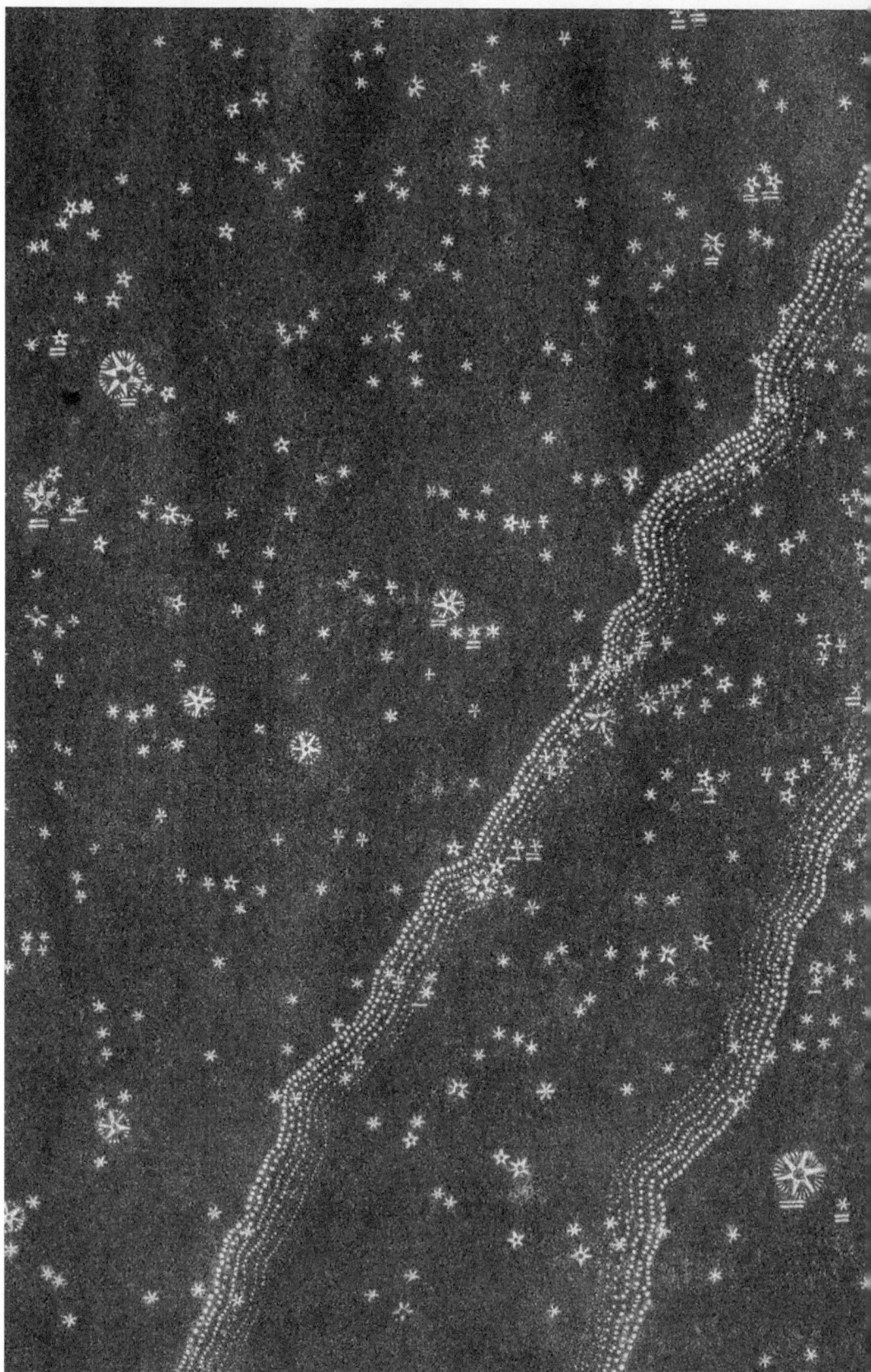

Autumn leaves drop from trees and fly
Forgotten like our dreams
Candles lit in silent prayer
Where once our wishes went
The chest of treasures we dived for
Still buried deep unfound....

Hopes and visions from summers gone
Frozen by winter's melody
Laughter and joy from our field of dreams
Echoes in a lost horizon

Goals and aspirations cry to fly
Like birds with broken wings
Failure with heartache from unattained purpose
Floating painfully down memory's enraptured river

LOST

They came through you, not from you said the prophet
So our prayed for children
We stand still as the bow
And on your flight, find the story already written
It is in the glorious morning sky
In that moment within when we let go

Remember your sweet innocence
See the glistening first dew
Embrace the wonder
Smell the lilacs too
Witness the miracle
And feel the love

Before you forget who you are
Be not what they want
Be true son and daughter
Then and ONLY then you are YOU

ENLIGHTENED

Leaving you was a fork in the road
Where my life went one way
And my dreams went another
My castles too fell from the sky
Leaving only the shells of hope
Scattered around like so much debris
But I dusted myself off and began walking
Telling myself I wouldn't chase them
Yet believing that, like a long lost friend
My dreams and I would one day meet again.

And there she floats into a world of crimson sunsets
Where anything is possible and nothing awry

And she leaves behind landslides of tears
Children yet to adult

And she feels the burden lifting
Though one last glance is painful

And she extends her hand to be pulled up to resting
Then they embrace her — all those gone long ago

And hence they came.... Her grandmother's sweet breath welcoming
Vivling in all her mesmerizing allure, friends long gone now giggling,
The child she never knew now knowing, and that one imagined love.

LEAVING

Worthlessness washes ashore yet again
Not calm but a thrashing
Like a million arrows it pierces my existence
Constant without rest
I wonder where the meaning is
Where a light is supposed to guide
Has been extinguished
Here rolls in the first thoughts of
Darkness as I descend

DARKNESS

When your heart is heavy
You do not know but,
I carry it too
When your hands are empty
When your soul is weary

When your mind is racing
When your fears are unyielding
You are not alone
I am with you

Seduce me with the words you whispered in my ear
The portrait you paint of my flight
Come to me in my dreams of Never Land
When I only think of you,
 in the darkness of my aloneness

Seduce me with pictures you help me imagine
The scent in a field of wild roses
Come to me in my baby's breath
When the pain of past losses,
 shatters my beating heart

Seduce me with visions of our minds entwining
The kiss to take my life's meaning
Come to me in the seconds before my last blink
When the final flickering image,
 is of your saving grace

Seduce me with images of yesterday's nostalgia
The message that awakens my sleeping soul
Come to me as the words to this story seem lost
When you have ripped apart,
My deserving logic

Seduce me again with past pleasures
The story of their doomed romance
Come to me in words they exchanged, now dusty archives
When through their lives,
we make our travels

Seduce me with one last imaginary kiss
The longing glance I dream you'll give
Come to me with flowers you might've picked
When the gold edged diary,
Over flows with our love

SEDUCTION

I love you like the sun loves the day
Like the moon loves the night
I love you when the sky turns dark
And in the early morning light

To feel your lips against my own
I would accept months of sorrow
To hold you in my arms just once
I would bear more pain tomorrow

Lay your hands all over me
I cannot wait, make haste
Tattoo my body with your lips
Leave a mark that wont erase

I need you like the air to breathe
Like water to survive
I need you more than anything else
You make me feel alive

Once when I adored you
You lifted me to Everest
Sunday's goodbye turned to Monday's hello

Once when you looked at me
With your brown lustful eyes
I smiled back and we nearly touched

Once when you were eager
To teach me all that was right
I felt I had wings and the world was incredible

Once is now when you walk past
And I am totally invisible
I wish the breaths you take inhaled me

Once is now when I hear
You speak to an insignificant other
I wish that hearing you made me deaf

Once is now when you cease
To acknowledge my existence
I wish I could grasp the wind caressing your shirt

Once is now as I erase these words
Scrubbing hard to regain my dignity
I wish the madness you imprinted vanishes

ONCE & NOW

Once I thought I had you
I grasped at the edge of your coat
But you slipped through my fingers

Once I thought I heard you
In the melody of a voice
But the notes they blew away in the wind

Once I thought I saw you
Flashing briefly in my lover's eyes
But just a blink and you had vanished

Once I thought I felt you
In a soft caress of my skin
But then your hand grew cold

Once I thought I glimpsed you
Walking far ahead of me
But though I ran I could not catch you

Once I thought I found you
Standing right in front of me
But then I woke, for you were just a dream

A shadow, a whisper

Oh love, elusive love

A desire like a thousand windswept storms
  They chased passion like running after rain

Clinging to a frivolous all consuming embrace
Clearing to a blossoming day
  Canopied by a mythical rainbow

To be surpassed by the blinding light of tomorrow
And eclipsed by the gloom
  Of a jealous ominous cloud

Leaving their sketch on love's legendary landscape
For mortals to dream of
  And that was their love

DARLINGS OF GODS

I took a wrong turn
And ended up on memory lane
I met the person I used to be
Stars in my eyes and heart so naïve

I saw you there and my heart did miss you
The person I thought you were when I kissed you
Before all your lies were revealed
Before my eyes were unveiled

It's tempting to linger here and wonder
Why you tore my heart asunder
But I cannot stay here on memory lane
Holding onto ghosts in vain

The reflection I see is not who I was
All those years ago when you had my heart
But then it was I that fooled myself
Believing in an illusion

An image you could not live up to
I was in love with someone else
Created and nurtured by my youthful imagination
The only outcome was shattering reality

NAIVITY

Let me summon these winds to carry my forbidden words
In a chariot to you over the Caspian Sea......I love you.

DESIROUS SEA

My love, my tears, my desires, my pain
They are floating and thrashing and trying to catch their breath
For I am all sea
And they are the shipwrecks I tried to keep concealed

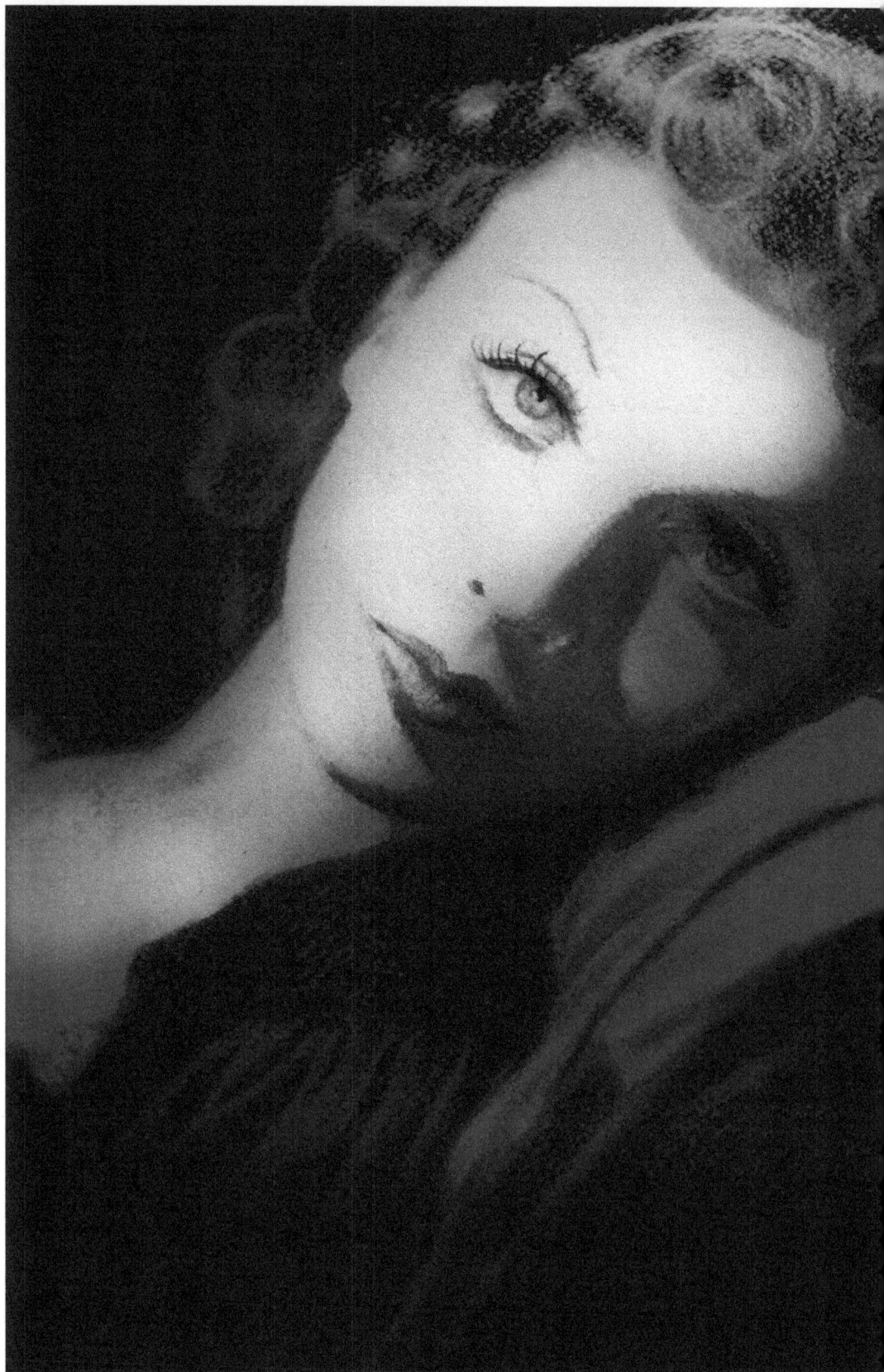

Quivering patterns of another tomorrow fade away,
But my love for you stays eternal,
        ethereal angel from another time.
The bewitching charm behind the mesh,
Perfection veiled and promising,
Then the tinkle of the Chinese lantern,
when she smiles…..illuminating my life.

VIVIEN

A sorceress that cast her spell
With dancing eyes like whirlpools of aquamarine

ENCHANTRESS

There are tattoos of your lips
All over my body
That only I can see

Sometimes you leave a mark on my skin
And in my mind remains the image of your face
But the imprint you've made on my heart.....
Will be the hardest to erase

They say tomorrow never comes
So tomorrow I'll lay my cards on the table
And speak the words I've never been able
I love you, I need you, I want you, I care
My most treasured moments are the ones that we've shared

I want to hand over my heart for your keeping
I want to be the one you've spent a lifetime seeking
I know this life we're all living is borrowed
So I won't keep it a secret,
I'll tell you...
Tomorrow

What a pleasure it is to be acquainted with your lips,
Which once were strangers to me

These thoughts of you
Are always on my mind
These thoughts of you
Come to me, unbidden
When I'm driving here
When I'm walking there

These thoughts of you
Come to me, unwanted
When I close my eyes at night
When I open them in the morning
Sometimes I wish I could siphon out
These thoughts of you
And pour them down the drain

A hiding sun playing with a bleak day
Carpeted by a sea of chalcedony
Salty air moistening my lips
This moment's peace belongs only to me

Crashing sea, foreboding an eerie emptiness
Song of the winds welcomes a symphony of mist
As she settles on the sea face like a veil landing

Solitude......
        Only one comes to mind in my solitude

    SOLITUDE

Nestled in her warm embrace
Rain falls heavily outside
disturbing rolling plains of tea shrubs
I am 4 again

Broad forehead, black hair crimpled ala flapper
Slender eyebrows, thin aquiline nose
Bow like sweet lips teaching me my first words
Talented hands guiding my hand to trace

When Grandpa's laughter stopped one day
I was growing up in Aoteroa
The flute played by the monk in the far away
temple
continued a melancholy tune

The fragrance of incense upright in bronze holders
floated through the bungalow
When I went back to comfort her
I was by then 18

LEELA KUMARI

You were an angel passing briefly through this world.
As you passed through, you showed such wisdom, such kindness,
such enlightenment.
A higher level of consciousness so rarely seen.
You held yourself with such dignity and exuded so much gentleness.
Giving so much and expecting little in return.
You'll never know how much you have influenced me in your wake.
Your memory makes me strive to continue on this path that you forged…
To do right when it isn't easy, to stay courageous in the face of adversity,
To believe that karma comes to you in the afterlife and not in this life.

My heart runs over
Like an overfilled glass
Spilling everywhere
Staining everything
Try as I might to soak it up
It won't lift, it only fades
You only need to look closely
To see the blemish remains
I try but alas, all in vain
As I cannot remove
The remnants of love

Did we run into a burning house
to save something once loved?
Did we give it all a second chance?
Passions once obsessed over now saved
But here we are trapped
Engulfed by smoke of torture
Lost in a competitive madness
Waiting to be saved ourselves

BURNT

The person who has your heart, does not value you
And here I am silently, dying to give you the world.

⊥⊥

The words I want to say die on my lips.
Afraid my eyes will betray me, I turn away,
As though you are the sun and I've gazed upon you too long.
I fool myself that my feelings will set.
But like the sun, I reawaken to them each day.

⊥⊥

Deep within me there is a lake
Where eternal hope floats
And in my memories the scent of the love I lost

FLAME

In this pond of enchantment lies
Tickerage winds blowing melody of heartbreaks
Leaves rustling, echoing her sweet laughter
Bluebells yonder woods swaying like her slender hips
And she sleeps at long last with
water lilies as her crown

TICKERAGE LAKE

One day I'll find all the pieces of my soul that are missing, that are hidden inside other people; in experiences, and moments, and books. Perhaps some I'll stumble upon in distant lands, and others where I'd never thought to look. My mother bestowed an important one upon me at my birth. And I've already found a piece of my soul in an angel passing briefly through this earth. I know some are revealed through heartbreak and others in the lyrics of a song. While compassion towards others is the key to unlocking what has been within me all along. I know my journey is far from complete and there's no map for the missing pieces. But I know my life's purpose is to keep searching until my time on earth ceases.

My words will leave pieces of me
Reflections from the windows of my soul
There are tears of longing, songs for the gone
Hymns for peace, feelings unlocked
Droplets from sadness spilt,
Soft bare footed footsteps taken on rain-washed tiles
Deafening silence of love unexpressed
Odes to heroes, invisible feelings
Scribbles on Ceylon's red soil
Cosmic mysteries not yet explained
Undying adoration for the cherubs
Whispers from times gone
The warmth emanated from grandma's embrace
Aches for lost loves whom I never met
Travels with Castor through the constellation
And tucked away secret smiles for dreams yet to
come.....

WORDS

You are a book I want to read every day
I will not ever put you down
I want to fall asleep with you on my chest
And wake up early to read the next chapter
I won't miss a word
No I will not skip a line
Because I want to know everything there is to know
You're a mystery
Each time I turn a leaf
Your character becomes more vivid
More beautiful
I want to read you every day
Until the pages are creased

Part of me wants to wax lyrical to anyone who'll listen
about how perfect you are
How your smile is brighter than the northern lights
How your embrace gets me through the coldest nights
How the sound of your voice makes me shiver with anticipation
How every moment with you feels like a celebration
But the other part of me wants to keep it a secret
So everyone else doesn't fall in love with you too

You're like a glass of wine
The more I have the more I want
You're smooth on my lips
And I close my eyes to savour you
You enter my bloodstream
And suddenly I can't think clearly
You're like a glass of wine
You go straight to my head

You taste better than the first sip of wine......

You are the lines of my favorite poem
The lyrics to my favorite song
So let me love you when you're weak
Not only when you're strong
I want to be by your side when your heart is broken
Hear the words you can speak and those left unspoken
Please don't feel you must hide any part of who you are
Because I only love more when you show me your scars

My darling, tell me your story
Show me the wounds
Read aloud to me each chapter
Include the end
Reveal to me the beauty you hide
The love your afraid to give
Uncover to me your cuts
And then I'll still love **you**
And you'll see love through love's eyes

SCARS

This moment, this precious moment……
When true love shines through your gorgeous eyes
I know for certain you're mine
When the past does not enter the equation
And I see clearly life's meaning
When the wounds we inflicted suddenly heal
And we are without the stain of betrayal
When in our innocence all was perfect

Quick catch it before it vanishes……

MOMENTS

You and I my twin, we won't get marked in history
Nor engraved in stone
Or sung about

But here in a poem
A sentence
In between a stanza, the flick of a page, a word,
And a breath
Maybe someone might remember us

REMEMBRANCE

Perfect would be laying in bed with you
The sound of rain falling heavy on the roof
Close together, my skin against your skin
Your scent like heaven, breathing you in
No clocks in this room, time standing still
Ask me to stay like this always, I will

Here Castor, hold the mirror to me
So I can see the reverse of my reflection
The negatives and positives
Our dual personalities
A dash here, a sprinkle there

Oh Castor, this cold trickster planet
Rules over us with no mercy
Forcing us to try on many masks
We simply can't keep discarding them
In our endless search for ourselves

Maybe Castor, somewhere beneath our faces
When mental, spiritual and physical harmonize
I'll ride that silver chariot across the galaxy
And finally, I Pollux, will find my passion

Listen Castor, put away your fidgeting
Hear Mercury trine at twilight
Then the caterpillar will become the winged butterfly
And finally, you Castor, will find your identity!

GEMINI TO GEMINI

Artwork of Vivien Leigh courtesy Alejandro Franks